When the War Came

Sheila Hollins & Sue Carmichael
illustrated by Lucyna Talejko-Kwiatkowska

Beyond Words

London

14

First published in the UK 2023 by Books Beyond Words.

Text & illustrations © Books Beyond Words, 2023.

No part of this book may be reproduced in any form, or by any means, without the prior permission in writing from the publisher.

ISBN 978-1-78458-156-5

British Library Cataloguing-in-Publication Data

A catalogue record for this book is available from the British Library.

Printed by Royal British Legion Industries, Leatherhead.

Books Beyond Words is a Charitable Incorporated Organisation (no. 1183942).

Further information about the Books Beyond Words series can be obtained from Beyond Words' website: www.booksbeyondwords.co.uk.

Acknowledgments

Many thanks to the Beyond Words Book Club members in Kent who held special sessions to trial the pictures (Cas, Ray, Dawn, Paul, Marc, Pia and Andrew), to children who attend Feelings Groups at Laithes School in Barnsley and to Larysa for bravely sharing her experience.

More Information

https://booksbeyondwords.co.uk/s/
When-the-War-Came-2023-for-
website.pdf